"Choose my instruction
instead of silver,
knowledge rather than
choice gold, for wisdom is
more precious than rubies,
and nothing you desire can
compare with her."
Proverbs 8:10,11 *(NIV)*

Pocket Proverbs

Wisdom to Live By

Pocket Proverbs

Wisdom to Live By

Over 450
Proverbs from the
Word of God

Chosen by
David Wilkerson

World Wide

A ministry of
the Billy Graham Association

1303 Hennepin Avenue
Minneapolis, Minnesota 55403

The translation of all Regal books is under the direction of GLINT. GLINT provides technical help for the adaptation, translation and publishing of books for millions of people worldwide. For information regarding translation contact: GLINT, P.O. Box 6688, Ventura, California 93006.

Scripture quotations in this publication are from the following versions:
TLB—The Living Bible, Copyright © 1971 by Tyndale House Publishers, Wheaton, Illinois. Used by permission.
NIV—New International Version, Holy Bible. Copyright © 1973 and 1978 by New York International Bible Society. Used by permission.

Published by Permission of Regal Books
A Division of GL Publications
Ventura, California 93006
Printed in U.S.A.

Library of Congress Cataloging in Publication data

Bible. English. Selections. 1983.
    Pocket proverbs.
    Includes index.
    I. Wilkerson, David. R. II. Title.
BS391.2.W54 1983   220.5'2   83-3405
ISBN 0-8307-0893-6

Contents

16. Don't be afraid of calamities or world disasters.
17. Learn the true meaning of life and how to be fulfilled.
18. Don't ever co-sign any notes or loans.
19. Don't get addicted to sleep.
20. Avoid the things which God hates.
21. Learn the horrific consequences of adultery.
22. Trust God for all things.
23. Avoid gossip like a plague. Don't spread rumors.
24. Seek good counsel before acting on any matter.
25. Don't hoard food.
26. Encourage people who are hurting and depressed—but do it intelligently.
27. Don't believe everything you hear.
28. Bring your temper under control before you destroy everything in your life.
29. Reverence God as the one true source of character growth.
30. Develop a relaxed, joyful attitude toward life.
31. Stay hungry for truth.
32. Don't try to prove you are right.
33. Commit everything in your life to God's care.

34. Never gloat when your enemies suffer. Never seek revenge.
35. Look past mistakes in others.
36. Always be loyal to your friends. Enjoy them.
37. Stubbornness is a satanic trait—learn to submit.
38. Always keep an open mind.
39. Don't rush into things—go slow and be sure.
40. Develop a spirit of kindness.
41. Never, never get involved in other people's quarrels.
42. Learn to shut up and listen.
43. Learn to save.
44. Avoid ungodly friends.
45. Don't be envious of the prosperity of others.
46. Put God's work first—above all personal needs.
47. Bless your enemies and harbor no ill will.
48. Control your appetites before they control you.
49. Don't be fooled by flattery.
50. Jealousy is cancerous; destroy it entirely.
51. Never fear what man can do to you.

52. Don't lie on your bed at night fretting about problems.
53. Learn to be content with what you have.
54. Be patient.
55. Allow no fear in your life.
56. Think of death without fearing it.
57. If God is prospering you—don't feel guilty.
58. Don't judge anyone by appearances or by what he believes.
59. Never criticize—that is destructive to all growth.
60. Try to be at peace with all men.
61. Keep your thought life under control.
62. Never let the cares of this life rob you of peace.
63. Allow no anger to rule your spirit.
64. Keep believing that God will give you the sanctified desires of your heart.
65. Don't be afraid of failing God—or falling.
66. Accept the forgiveness of the Lord.
67. God heals broken hearts of those who have childlike trust in Him.
68. Convince yourself that God is hearing your prayers.
69. Keep your courage up when things get bad.

Index

Introduction

This book is published with a warning against *Bibliomancy*—that is, using the Bible as a kind of divination, selecting Bible verses at random to predict future events. Bibliomancy consists in dipping into the Bible as if it were a magician's hat and pulling out directives and quickie solutions for problems. This, all too often, is what people do with Scripture Cards.

Scripture Cards (later known as Promise Cards) were introduced in the early 1800s. Adam Clarke called them "the scandal of Christianity," because certain believers, choosing at random Scripture Cards that threatened awful judgments, were driven to despair regarding the future state of their souls. To combat the "judgment cards," John Wesley was credited with printing cards containing nothing but the most comfortable promises. The Methodists of that era denied Wesley printed such cards; however they became very popular in his societies. The secular press of the day referred to these cards as the "sacred lottery."

This book of proverbs is not a sacred lottery. Rather, it consists of solid promises or exhortations that are repeated over and over. That is why I have included at least four Bible verses under each heading. My grandfather told me that since builders never build on a foundation of one or two walls, I should find at least four verses (walls) upon which to build every important truth.

Remember that divine guidance seldom comes through random Bible verses. The Spirit has promised to lead us into *all* truth, but this does not suggest that guidance and truth are given *only* by divine revelation. The Spirit may lead someone to give us an inspired book; some praying friend may be directed to us with a word of sound wisdom and counsel; and, most often, the Spirit will confirm what we need to know, and often what we have already heard inwardly, by numerous Bible verses.

Having warned against the misuse of Bible verses, let me encourage you in the right use. Every promise and proverb is yours—every jot and tittle. Study them prayerfully and believe that the Spirit will open their deepest meaning to you. Never be afraid to use these Bible verses as a sword to bring down the strongholds of Satan.

At times, a single verse is made very real to you. It becomes "your verse—your word." It becomes as real as if God Himself had visited you in person to deliver it. Don't be afraid to claim it once the Spirit enlightens it to you.

I suggest you memorize as many verses as possible, because this is the wisdom of God that, once hidden in your heart, will continuously produce godly character.

1. Learn to take reproof, advice, criticism.

Do not rebuke a mocker or he will hate you; rebuke a wise man and he will love you. Instruct a wise man and he will be wiser still; teach a righteous man and he will add to his learning—*Proverbs 9:8-9, NIV.*

Anyone willing to be corrected is on the pathway to life. Anyone refusing has lost his chance—*Proverbs 10:17, TLB.*

He who ignores discipline comes to poverty and shame, but whoever heeds correction is honored—*Proverbs 13:18, NIV.*

He who listens to a life-giving rebuke will be at home among the wise. He who ignores discipline despises himself, but whoever heeds correction gains understanding—*Proverbs 15:31-32, NIV.*

In the end, people appreciate frankness more than flattery—*Proverbs 28:23, TLB.*

Don't refuse to accept criticism; get all the help you can—*Proverbs 23:12, TLB.*

Timely advice is as lovely as golden apples in a silver basket. It is a badge of honor to accept valid criticism—*Proverbs 25:11-12, TLB.*

A man who remains stiff-necked after many rebukes will suddenly be destroyed—without remedy—*Proverbs 29:1, NIV.*

Whoever loves discipline loves knowledge, but he who hates correction is stupid—*Proverbs 12:1, NIV.*

Only a fool despises his father's advice; a wise son considers each suggestion—*Proverbs 15:5, TLB.*

When a mocker is punished, the simple gain wisdom; when a wise man is instructed, he gets knowledge—*Proverbs 21:11, NIV.*

Listen to advice and accept instruction, and in the end you will be wise—*Proverbs 19:20, NIV.*

Punish a mocker and others will learn from his example. Reprove a wise man and he will be the wiser—*Proverbs 19:25, TLB.*

2. Learn to weigh all conversation before answering.

The mouth of the righteous is a fountain of life, but violence overwhelms the mouth of the wicked. Hatred stirs up dissension, but love covers over all wrongs—*Proverbs 10:11-12, NIV.*

Don't talk so much. You keep putting your foot in your mouth. Be sensible and turn off the flow! *Proverbs 10:19, TLB.*

When a good man speaks, he is worth listening to, but the words of fools are a dime a dozen. A godly man gives good advice, but a rebel is destroyed by lack of common sense—*Proverbs 10:20-21, TLB.*

The upright speak what is helpful; the wicked speak rebellion—*Proverbs 10:32, TLB.*

Evil words destroy. Godly skill rebuilds—
Proverbs 11:9, TLB.

Reckless words pierce like a sword, but the tongue of the wise brings healing—*Proverbs 12:18, NIV.*

He who ignores discipline despises himself, but whoever heeds correction gains understanding—*Proverbs 15:32, NIV.*

A good man thinks before he speaks; the evil man pours out his evil words without a thought—*Proverbs 15:28, TLB.*

A wise man's heart guides his mouth, and his lips promote instruction—*Proverbs 16:23, NIV.*

Those who love to talk will suffer the consequences. Men have died for saying the wrong thing! *Proverbs 18:21, TLB.*

A witness who tells the truth saves good men from being sentenced to death, but a false witness is a traitor—*Proverbs 14:25, TLB.*

The tongue that brings healing is a tree of life, but a deceitful tongue crushes the spirit—*Proverbs 15:4, NIV.*

You know what I am going to say before I even say it—*Psalm 139:4, TLB.*

Steer clear of foolish discussions which lead people into the sin of anger with each other—*2 Timothy 2:16, TLB.*

Your conversation should be so sensible and logical that anyone who wants to argue will be ashamed of himself because there won't be anything to criticize in anything you say!—*Titus 2:8, TLB.*

Do not be quick with your mouth, do not be hasty in your heart to utter anything before God. God is in heaven and you are on earth, so let your words be few—*Ecclesiastes 5:2, NIV.*

3. Be slow to speak. Be soft-spoken.

To quarrel with a neighbor is foolish; a man with good sense holds his tongue—*Proverbs 11:12, TLB.*

An evil man is trapped by his sinful talk, but a righteous man escapes trouble—*Proverbs 12:13, NIV.*

Self-control means controlling the tongue! A quick retort can ruin everything—*Proverbs 13:3, TLB.*

A gentle answer turns away wrath, but a harsh word stirs up anger—*Proverbs 15:1, NIV.*

The tongue that brings healing is a tree of life, but a deceitful tongue crushes the spirit—*Proverbs 15:4, NIV.*

Kind words are like honey—enjoyable and healthful—*Proverbs 16:24, TLB.*

The man of few words and settled mind is wise; therefore, even a fool is thought to be wise when he is silent. It pays him to keep his mouth shut—*Proverbs 17:27-28, TLB.*

A fool gets into constant fights. His mouth is his undoing! His words endanger him—*Proverbs 18:6-7, TLB.*

The quiet words of the wise are more to be heeded than the shouts of a ruler of fools—*Ecclesiastes 9:17, NIV.*

He who guards his mouth and his tongue keeps himself from calamity—*Proverbs 21:23, NIV.*

Do you see a man who speaks in haste? There is more hope for a fool than for him—*Proverbs 29:20, NIV.*

If the boss is angry with you, don't quit! A quiet spirit will quiet his bad temper—*Ecclesiastes 10:4, TLB.*

4. Don't covet riches or prosperity. And if you get riches, don't trust in them.

Your riches won't help you on Judgment Day; only righteousness counts then—*Proverbs 11:4, TLB.*

Whoever trusts in his riches will fall, but the righteous will thrive like a green leaf—*Proverbs 11:28, NIV.*

Better a little with reverence for God, than great treasure and trouble with it—*Proverbs 15:16, TLB.*

The Lord tears down the proud man's house but he keeps the widow's boundaries intact—*Proverbs 15:25, NIV.*

Better poor and humble than proud and rich—*Proverbs 16:19, TLB.*

The wealth of the rich is their fortified city; they imagine it an unscalable wall—*Proverbs 18:11, NIV.*

Do not wear yourself out to get rich; have the wisdom to show restraint. Cast but a glance at riches, and they are gone, for they will surely sprout wings and fly off to the sky like an eagle—*Proverbs 23:4-5, NIV.*

Better to be poor and honest than rich and a cheater—*Proverbs 28:6, TLB.*

A stingy man is eager to get rich and is unaware that poverty awaits him—*Proverbs 28:22, NIV.*

Two things I ask of you, O Lord; do not refuse me before I die: Keep falsehood and lies far from me; give me neither poverty nor riches, but give me only my daily bread. Otherwise, I may have too much and disown you and say, "Who is the Lord?" Or I may become poor and steal, and so dishonor the name of my God—*Proverbs 30:7-9, NIV.*

They trust in their wealth and boast about how rich they are, yet not one of them, though rich as kings, can ransom his own brother from the penalty of sin! For God's forgiveness does not come that way—*Psalm 49:6-7, TLB.*

Don't become rich by extortion and robbery. And don't let the rich men be proud—*Psalm 62:10-11, TLB.*

Whoever loves money never has money enough; whoever loves wealth is never satisfied with his income. This too is meaningless. As goods increase, so do those who consume them. And what benefit are they to the owner except to feast his eyes on them? The sleep of a laborer is sweet, whether he eats little or much, but the abundance of a rich man permits him no sleep—*Ecclesiastes 5:10-12, NIV.*

5. Always be compassionate to the poor.

Do not withhold good from those who deserve it, when it is in your power to act. Do not say to your neighbor, "Come back later; I'll give it tomorrow"—when you now have it with you—*Proverbs 3:27-28, NIV.*

He who despises his neighbor sins, but blessed is he who is kind to the needy—*Proverbs 14:21, NIV.*

Anyone who oppresses the poor is insulting God who made them. To help the poor is to honor God—*Proverbs 14:31, TLB.*

When you help the poor you are lending to the Lord—and he pays wonderful interest on your loan! *Proverbs 19:17, TLB.*

If a man shuts his ears to the cry of the poor, he too will cry out and not be answered—*Proverbs 21:13, NIV.*

He who gives to the poor will lack nothing, but he who closes his eyes to them receives many curses—*Proverbs 28:27, NIV.*

The righteous care about justice for the poor, but the wicked have no such concern—*Proverbs 29:7, NIV.*

You should defend those who cannot help themselves. Yes, speak up for the poor and needy, and see that they get justice—*Proverbs 31:8-9, TLB.*

A king who is fair to the poor shall have a long reign—*Proverbs 29:14, TLB.*

Blessed is he who has regard for the weak; the Lord delivers him in times of trouble—*Psalm 41:1, NIV.*

Defend the cause of the weak and father-less; maintain the rights of the poor and oppressed. Rescue the weak and needy; deliver them from the hand of the wicked— *Psalm 82:3-4, NIV.*

6. Learn the secrets to longer life.

My son, never forget the things I've taught you. If you want a long and satisfying life, closely follow my instructions—*Proverbs 3:1-2, TLB.*

Blessed is the man who finds wisdom, the man who gains understanding . . . . She is a tree of life to those who embrace her; those who lay hold of her will be blessed—*Proverbs 3:13,18, NIV.*

The fear of the Lord is the beginning of wisdom, and knowledge of the Holy One is understanding. For through me your days will be many, and years will be added to your life—*Proverbs 9:10-11, NIV.*

The fear of the Lord adds length to life, but the years of the wicked are cut short— *Proverbs 10:7, NIV.*

True humility and respect for the Lord lead a man to riches, honor and long life— *Proverbs 22:4, TLB.*

Do you want a long, good life? Then watch your tongue! Keep your lips from lying. Turn from all known sin and spend your time in doing good. Try to live in peace with everyone; work hard at it— *Psalm 34:12-14, TLB.*

Listen, my son, accept what I say, and the years of your life will be many— *Proverbs 4:10, NIV.*

7. Don't argue or quarrel with anyone. Agree with your adversary.

If you are looking for advice, stay away from fools— *Proverbs 14:7, TLB.*

If a wise man goes to court with a fool, the fool rages and scoffs, and there is no peace— *Proverbs 29:9, NIV.*

It is to a man's honor to avoid strife, but every fool is quick to quarrel— *Proverbs 20:3, NIV.*

When arguing with a rebel, don't use foolish arguments as he does, or you will become as foolish as he is! Prick his conceit with silly replies! *Proverbs 26:4-5, TLB.*

A fool gives full vent to his anger, but a wise man keeps himself under control— *Proverbs 29:11, NIV.*

An angry man stirs up dissension, and a hot-tempered one commits many sins— *Proverbs 29:22, NIV.*

Don't quarrel with anyone. Be at peace with everyone, just as much as possible— *Romans 12:18, TLB.*

Don't waste time arguing over foolish ideas and silly myths and legends. Spend your time and energy in the exercise of keeping spiritually fit— *1 Timothy 4:7, TLB.*

8. Be liberal; learn the power of giving.

A generous man will prosper; he who refreshes others will himself be refreshed— *Proverbs 11:25, NIV.*

Many beg favors from a man who is generous; everyone is his friend— *Proverbs 19:6, TLB.*

Happy is the generous man, the one who feeds the poor—*Proverbs 22:9, TLB.*

The wages of the righteous bring them life but the income of the wicked brings them punishment—*Proverbs 10:16, NIV.*

The lazy man longs for many things but his hands refuse to work. He is greedy to get, while the godly love to give!—*Proverbs 21:25-26, TLB.*

Give generously, for your gifts will return to you later. Divide your gifts among many, for in the days ahead you yourself may need much help—*Ecclesiastes 11:1-2, TLB.*

Remember this: Whoever sows sparingly will also reap sparingly, and whoever sows generously will also reap generously—*2 Corinthians 9:6, NIV.*

If you give, you will get! Your gift will return to you in full and overflowing measure, pressed down, shaken together to make room for more, and running over. Whatever measure you use to give—large or small—will be used to measure what is given back to you—*Luke 6:38, TLB.*

9. Don't brag on yourself.

If you have been a fool by being proud or plotting evil, don't brag about it—cover your mouth with your hand in shame—*Proverbs 30:32, TLB.*

Do not be wise in your own eyes; fear the Lord and shun evil—*Proverbs 3:7, NIV.*

The way of a fool seems right to him, but a wise man listens to advice—*Proverbs 12:15, NIV.*

There is one thing worse than a fool, and that is a man who is conceited—*Proverbs 26:12, TLB.*

A rich man may be wise in his own eyes, but a poor man who has discernment sees through him—*Proverbs 28:11, NIV.*

Hear their insolence! See their arrogance! How these men of evil boast! . . . Fools! Is God deaf and blind—he who makes ears and eyes? He punishes the nations—won't he also punish you? He knows everything—doesn't he also know what you are doing?—*Psalm 94:4,8-10, TLB.*

As God's messenger I give each of you God's warning: Be honest in your estimate of yourselves, measuring your value by how much faith God has given you—*Romans 12:3, TLB.*

10. Hate pride in any form.

Proud men end in shame, but the meek become wise—*Proverbs 11:2, TLB.*

Pride leads to arguments; be humble, take advice and become wise—*Proverbs 13:10, TLB.*

Pride goes before destruction, a haughty spirit before a fall—*Proverbs 16:18, NIV.*

Before his downfall a man's heart is proud, but humility comes before honor—*Proverbs 18:12, NIV.*

Pride ends in a fall, while humility brings honor—*Proverbs 29:23, TLB.*

To fear the Lord is to hate evil; I hate pride and arrogance, evil behavior and perverse speech—*Proverbs 8:13, NIV.*

The Lord tears down the proud man's house but he keeps the widow's boundaries intact—*Proverbs 15:25, NIV.*

Sinners love to fight; boasting is looking for trouble—*Proverbs 17:19, TLB.*

Pride, lust, and evil actions are all sin. Mockers are proud, haughty and arrogant—*Proverbs 21:4,24, TLB.*

Like clouds and wind without rain is a man who boasts of gifts he does not give. It is not good to eat too much honey, nor is it honorable to seek one's own honor—*Proverbs 25:14,27, NIV.*

Though [God] is so great, he respects the humble, but proud men must keep their distance—*Psalm 138:6, TLB.*

11. Avoid alcohol.

And it is not for kings, O Lemuel, to drink wine and whiskey. For if they drink they may forget their duties and be unable to give justice to those who are oppressed—*Proverbs 31:4-5, TLB.*

Wine is a mocker and beer a brawler; whoever is led astray by them is not wise—*Proverbs 20:1, NIV.*

A man who loves pleasure becomes poor; wine and luxury are not the way to riches!—*Proverbs 21:17, TLB.*

Don't let the sparkle and the smooth taste of strong wine deceive you. For in the end it bites like a poisonous serpent; it stings like an adder. You will see hallucinations and have delirium tremens, and you will say foolish, silly things that would embarrass you no end when sober. You will stagger like a sailor tossed at sea, clinging to a swaying mast. And afterwards you will say, "I didn't even know it when they beat me up . . . . Let's go and have another drink!"—*Proverbs 23:31-35, TLB.*

Whose heart is filled with anguish and sorrow? Who is always fighting and quarreling? Who is the man with bloodshot eyes and many wounds? It is the one who spends long hours in the taverns, trying out new mixtures—*Proverbs 23:29-30, TLB.*

It is better not to eat meat or drink wine or to do anything else that will cause your brother to fall—*Romans 14:21, NIV.*

12. Don't trust your own plans or wisdom.

Trust the Lord completely; don't ever trust yourself—*Proverbs 3:5, TLB.*

We can make our plans, but the final outcome is in God's hands—*Proverbs 16:1, TLB.*

We toss the coin, but it is the Lord who controls its decision—*Proverbs 16:33, TLB.*

Many are the plans in a man's heart, but it is the Lord's purpose that prevails—*Proverbs 19:21, NIV.*

A man's steps are directed by the Lord. How then can anyone understand his own way? *Proverbs 20:24, NIV.*

There is no wisdom, no insight, no plan that can succeed against the Lord. The horse is made ready for the day of battle, but victory rests with the Lord—*Proverbs 21:30-31, NIV.*

A man is a fool to trust himself! But those who use God's wisdom are safe—*Proverbs 28:26, TLB.*

It is better to trust the Lord than to put confidence in men. It is better to take refuge in him than in the mightiest king!—*Psalms 118:8-9. TLB.*

13. Seek direction from the Lord.

In all your ways acknowledge him, and he will make your paths straight—*Proverbs 3:6, NIV.*

We should make plans—counting on God to direct us—*Proverbs 16:9, TLB.*

What a shame—yes, how stupid!—to decide before knowing the facts!—*Proverbs 18:13, TLB.*

Lord, lead me as you promised me you would; otherwise my enemies will conquer me. Tell me clearly what to do, which way to turn—*Psalm 5:8, TLB.*

I walk in the way of righteousness, along the paths of justice—*Proverbs 8:20, NIV.*

The Lord gives wisdom, and from his mouth come knowledge and understanding. He holds victory in store for the upright, he is a shield to those whose walk is blameless, for he guards the course of the just and protects the way of his faithful ones— *Proverbs 2:6-8, NIV.*

The Lord delights in the way of the man whose steps he has made firm; though he stumble, he will not fall, for the Lord upholds him with his hand—*Psalm 37:23-24, NIV.*

14. Acquire blessings and wealth only according to God's plan.

Honor the Lord by giving him the first part of all your income, and he will fill your barns with wheat and barley and overflow your wine vats with the finest wines—*Proverbs 3:9-10, TLB.*

Blessed is the man who finds wisdom, the man who gains understanding . . . . Long life is in her right hand; in her left hand are riches and honor—*Proverbs 3:13,16, NIV.*

Wealth from gambling quickly disappears, wealth from hard work grows—*Proverbs 13:11, TLB.*

All hard work brings a profit, but mere talk leads only to poverty—*Proverbs 14:23, NIV.*

To be wise is as good as being rich; in fact, it is better. You can get anything by either wisdom or money, but being wise has many advantages—*Ecclesiastes 7:11-12, TLB.*

A little, gained honestly, is better than great wealth gotten by dishonest means—*Proverbs 16:8, TLB.*

Better be poor and honest than rich and dishonest—*Proverbs 19:1, TLB.*

The plans of the diligent lead to profit as surely as haste leads to poverty—*Proverbs 21:5, NIV.*

If you must choose, take a good name rather than great riches; for to be held in loving esteem is better than silver and gold—*Proverbs 22:1, TLB.*

Do you know a hard-working man? He shall be successful and stand before kings! *Proverbs 22:29, TLB.*

He who works his land will have abundant food, but the one who chases fantasies will have his fill of poverty—*Proverbs 28:19, NIV.*

Greed causes fighting; trusting God leads to prosperity—*Proverbs 28:25, TLB.*

All who humble themselves before the Lord shall be given every blessing, and shall have wonderful peace—*Psalm 37:11, TLB.*

Praise the Lord! For all who fear God and trust in him are blessed beyond expression. Yes, happy is the man who delights in doing his commands. His children shall be honored everywhere, for good men's sons have a special heritage. He himself shall be wealthy, and his good deeds will never be forgotten—*Psalm 112:1-3, TLB.*

15. Don't be afraid of God's rod of correction.

My son, do not despise the Lord's discipline and do not resent his rebuke, because the Lord disciplines those he loves, as a father the son he delights in—*Proverbs 3:11-12, NIV.*

Blessed is the man you discipline, O Lord, the man you teach from your law; you grant him relief from days of trouble—*Psalm 94:12-13, NIV.*

Happy are those who are strong in the Lord, who want above all else to follow your steps. When they walk through the Valley of Weeping it will become a place of springs where pools of blessing and refreshment collect after rains!—*Psalm 84:5-6, TLB.*

You have given us your laws to obey— oh, how I want to follow them consistently. Then I will not be disgraced, for I will have a clean record. After you have corrected me I will thank you by living as I should! . . . I know, O Lord, that your decisions are right and that your punishment was right and did me good—*Psalm 119:4-7,75, TLB.*

Blessed is the man whom God corrects; so do not despise the discipline of the Almighty—*Job 5:17, NIV.*

16. Don't be afraid of calamities or world disasters.

Evil will slay the wicked; the foes of the righteous will be condemned. The Lord redeems his servants; no one who takes refuge in him will be condemned—*Psalm 34:21-22, NIV.*

The Lord saves the godly! He is their salvation and their refuge when trouble comes. Because they trust in him, he helps them and delivers them from the plots of evil men—*Psalm 37:39-40, TLB*.

You need not be afraid of disaster or the plots of wicked men, for the Lord is with you; he protects you—*Proverbs 3:25-26, TLB*.

The godly learn by watching ruin overtake the wicked—*Proverbs 21:12, TLB*.

Good will come to him who is generous and lends freely, who conducts his affairs with justice. Surely he will never be shaken; a righteous man will be remembered forever. He will have no fear of bad news; his heart is steadfast, trusting in the Lord—*Psalm 112:5-7, NIV*.

The Lord lives! Praise be to my Rock! Exalted be God my Savior! *Psalm 18:46, NIV*.

How dare you tell me, "Flee to the mountains for safety," when I am trusting in the Lord? For the wicked have strung their bows, drawn their arrows tight against the bowstrings, and aimed from ambush at the people of God. "Law and order have collapsed," we are told. "What can the righteous do but flee?" But the Lord is still in his holy temple; he still rules from heaven. He closely watches everything that happens here on earth—*Psalm 11:1-4, TLB.*

He is my strength, my shield from every danger. I trusted in him, and he helped me. Joy rises in my heart until I burst out in songs of praise to him. The Lord protects his people and gives victory to his anointed king. Defend your people, Lord; defend and bless your chosen ones. Lead them like a shepherd and carry them forever in your arms—*Psalm 28:7-9, TLB.*

God is our refuge and strength, an ever present help in trouble. Therefore we will not fear, though the earth give way and the mountains fall into the heart of the sea, though its waters roar and foam and the mountains quake with their surging. There is a river whose streams make glad the city of God, the holy place where the Most High dwells. God is within her, she will not fall; God will help her at break of day. Nations are in uproar, kingdoms fall; he lifts his voice, the earth melts. The Lord Almighty is with us; the God of Jacob is our fortress. Come and see the works of the Lord, the desolations he has brought on the earth. He makes wars cease to the ends of the earth; he breaks the bow and shatters the spear, he burns the shields with fire. "Be still, and know that I am God; I will be exalted among the nations, I will be exalted in the earth." The Lord Almighty is with us; the God of Jacob is our fortress—*Psalm 46, NIV.*

Oh, how great is your goodness to those who publicly declare that you will rescue them. For you have stored up great blessings for those who trust and reverence you. Hide your loved ones in the shelter of your presence, safe beneath your hand, safe from all conspiring men—*Psalm 31:19-20, TLB.*

Cheer up! Take courage if you are depending on the Lord—*Psalm 31:24, TLB.*

There is no need to fear when times of trouble come, even though surrounded by enemies!—*Psalm 49:5, TLB.*

The Lord is close to the brokenhearted and saves those who are crushed in spirit. A righteous man may have many troubles, but the Lord delivers him from them all; he protects all his bones, not one of them will be broken—*Psalm 34:18-20, NIV.*

17. Learn the true meaning of life and how to be fulfilled.

Hold on to instruction, do not let it go; guard it well, for it is your life—*Proverbs 4:13, NIV.*

Above all else, guard your heart, for it is the wellspring of life . . . . Make level paths for your feet and take only ways that are firm—*Proverbs 4:23,26, NIV.*

For their [your father's and your mother's] advice is a beam of light directed into the dark corners of your mind to warn you of danger and to give you a good life—*Proverbs 6:23, TLB.*

Anyone willing to be corrected is on the pathway to life. Anyone refusing has lost his chance—*Proverbs 10:17, TLB.*

The faithless will be fully repaid for their ways, and the good man rewarded for his—*Proverbs 14:14, NIV.*

The man who knows right from wrong and has good judgment and common sense is happier than the man who is immensely rich! For such wisdom is far more valuable than precious jewels. Nothing else compares with it—*Proverbs 3:13-15, TLB.*

Godliness with contentment is great gain—*1 Timothy 6:6, NIV.*

18. Don't ever co-sign any notes or loans.

Son, if you endorse a note for someone you hardly know, guaranteeing his debt, you are in serious trouble. You may have trapped yourself by your agreement. Quick! Get out of it if you possibly can! Swallow your pride; don't let embarrassment stand in the way. Go and beg to have your name erased. Don't put it off. Do it now. Don't rest until you do. If you can get out of this trap you have saved yourself like a deer that escapes from a hunter, or a bird from the net—*Proverbs 6:1-5, TLB.*

He who puts up security for another will surely suffer, but whoever refuses to strike hands in pledge is safe—*Proverbs 11:15, NIV.*

It is poor judgment to countersign another's note, to become responsible for his debts—*Proverbs 17:18, TLB.*

It is risky to make loans to strangers!—*Proverbs 20:16, TLB.*

Unless you have the extra cash on hand, don't countersign a note. Why risk everything you own? They'll even take your bed!—*Proverbs 22:26-27, TLB*.

Take the garment of one who puts up security for a stranger; hold it in pledge if he does it for a wayward woman—*Proverbs 27:13, NIV*.

19. Don't get addicted to sleep.

A little sleep, a little slumber, a little folding of the hands to rest—and poverty will come on you like a bandit and scarcity like an armed man—*Proverbs 6:10-11, NIV*.

A lazy man sleeps soundly—and goes hungry!—*Proverbs 19:15, TLB*.

If you love sleep, you will end in poverty. Stay awake, work hard, and there will be plenty to eat!—*Proverbs 20:13, TLB*.

O my son, be wise and stay in God's paths; don't carouse with drunkards and gluttons, for they are on their way to poverty. And remember that too much sleep clothes a man with rags—*Proverbs 23:19-21, TLB*.

The lazy man won't go out and work. "There might be a lion outside!" he says. He sticks to his bed like a door to its hinges! He is too tired even to lift his food from his dish to his mouth! Yet in his own opinion he is smarter than seven wise men—*Proverbs 26:13-16, TLB.*

Lazy hands make a man poor, but diligent hands bring wealth. He who gathers crops in summer is a wise son, but he who sleeps during harvest is a disgraceful son—*Proverbs 10:4-5, NIV.*

20. Avoid the things which God hates.

There are six things the Lord hates, seven that are detestable to him: haughty eyes, a lying tongue, hands that shed innocent blood, a heart that devises wicked schemes, feet that are quick to rush into evil, a false witness who pours out lies, and a man who stirs up dissension among brothers—*Proverbs 6:16-19, NIV.*

Work hard and become a leader; be lazy and never succeed—*Proverbs 12:24, TLB.*

I walked by the field of a certain lazy fellow and saw that it was overgrown with thorns, and covered with weeds; and its walls were broken down. Then, as I looked, I learned this lesson: "A little extra sleep, a little more slumber, a little folding of the hands to rest" means that poverty will break in upon you suddenly like a robber, and violently like a bandit—*Proverbs 24:30-34, TLB.*

Let those who love the Lord hate evil, for he guards the lives of his faithful ones and delivers them from the hand of the wicked—*Psalm 97:10, NIV.*

21. Learn the horrific consequences of adultery.

Do not lust in your heart after her beauty or let her captivate you with her eyes, for the prostitute reduces you to a loaf of bread, and the adulteress preys upon your very life. Can a man scoop fire into his lap without his clothes being burned? . . . So is he who sleeps with another man's wife; no one who touches her will go unpunished—*Proverbs 6:25-27,29, NIV.*

The man who commits adultery is an utter fool, for he destroys his own soul. Wounds and constant disgrace are his lot, for the woman's husband will be furious in his jealousy, and he will have no mercy on you in his day of vengeance. You won't be able to buy him off no matter what you offer—*Proverbs 6:32-35, TLB.*

Don't let your desires get out of hand; don't let yourself think about her. Don't go near her; stay away from where she walks, lest she tempt you and seduce you. For she has been the ruin of multitudes—a vast host of men have been her victims. If you want to find the road to hell, look for her house—*Proverbs 7:25-27, TLB.*

For the lips of an adulteress drip honey, and her speech is smoother than oil; but in the end she is bitter as gall, sharp as a double-edged sword. Her feet go down to death; her steps lead straight to the grave—*Proverbs 5:3-5, NIV.*

Run from her! Don't go near her house, lest you fall to her temptation and lose your honor, and give the remainder of your life to the cruel and merciless; lest strangers obtain your wealth, and you become a slave of foreigners. Lest afterwards you groan in anguish and in shame, when syphilis consumes your body, and you say, "Oh, if only I had listened! If only I had not demanded my own way! Oh, why wouldn't I take advice? Why was I so stupid?"—*Proverbs 5:8-13, TLB.*

Why be captivated, my son, by an adulteress? Why embrace the bosom of another man's wife? For a man's ways are in full view of the Lord, and he examines all his paths. The evil deeds of a wicked man ensnare him; the cords of his sin hold him fast. He will die for lack of discipline, led astray by his own great folly—*Proverbs 5:20-23, NIV.*

22. Trust God for all things.

The Lord will not let a good man starve to death, nor will he let the wicked man's riches continue forever—*Proverbs 10:3, TLB.*

Lord, you have assigned me my portion and my cup; you have made my lot secure—*Psalm 16:5, NIV.*

If you belong to the Lord, reverence him; for everyone who does this has everything he needs—*Psalm 34:9, TLB.*

A greedy man stirs up dissension, but he who trusts in the Lord will prosper—*Proverbs 28:25, NIV.*

Fear of man will prove to be a snare, but whoever trusts in the Lord is kept safe—*Proverbs 29:25, NIV.*

Every word of God proves true. He defends all who come to him for protection—*Proverbs 30:5, TLB.*

Delight yourself in the Lord and he will give you the desires of your heart. Commit your way to the Lord; trust in him and he will do this—*Psalm 37:4-5, NIV.*

What I want from you is your true thanks; I want your promises fulfilled. I want you to trust me in your times of trouble, so I can rescue you, and you can give me glory—*Psalm 50:14-15, TLB.*

My protection and success come from God alone. He is my refuge, a Rock where no enemy can reach me. O my people, trust him all the time. Pour out your longings before him, for he can help!—*Psalm 62:7-8, TLB.*

23. Avoid gossip like a plague. Don't spread rumors.

A gossip goes around spreading rumors, while a trustworthy man tries to quiet them—*Proverbs 11:13, TLB.*

An evil man sows strife; gossip separates the best of friends—*Proverbs 16:28, TLB.*

Don't tell your secrets to a gossip unless you want them broadcast to the world—*Proverbs 20:19, TLB.*

Like a club or a sword or a sharp arrow is the man who gives false testimony against his neighbor—*Proverbs 25:18, NIV.*

Without wood a fire goes out; without gossip a quarrel dies down—*Proverbs 26:20, NIV.*

Gossip is a dainty morsel eaten with great relish. Pretty words may hide a wicked heart, just as a pretty glaze covers a common clay pot—*Proverbs 26:22-23, TLB.*

The words of a gossip are like choice morsels; they go down to a man's inmost parts—*Proverbs 18:8, NIV.*

Lord, who may go and find refuge and shelter in your tabernacle up on your holy hill? Anyone who leads a blameless life and is truly sincere. Anyone who refuses to slander others, does not listen to gossip, never harms his neighbor—*Psalm 15:1-3, TLB.*

Do not pay attention to every word people say, or you may hear your servant cursing you—for you know in your heart that many times you yourself have cursed others—*Ecclesiastes 7:21-22, NIV.*

24. Seek good counsel before acting on any matter.

Without wise leadership, a nation is in trouble; but with good counselors there is safety—*Proverbs 11:14, TLB.*

Plans fail for lack of counsel, but with many advisers they succeed—*Proverbs 15:22, NIV.*

Though good advice lies deep within a counselor's heart, the wise man will draw it out—*Proverbs 20:5, TLB.*

Make plans by seeking advice; if you wage war, obtain guidance—*Proverbs 20:18, NIV.*

Pay attention and listen to the sayings of the wise; apply your heart to what I teach, for it is pleasing when you keep them in your heart and have all of them ready on your lips. So that your trust may be in the Lord, I teach you today, even you—*Proverbs 22:17-19, NIV.*

Don't go to war without wise guidance; there is safety in many counselors—*Proverbs 24:6, TLB.*

Let the wise listen and add to their learning, and let the discerning get guidance—*Proverbs 1:5, NIV.*

A fool thinks he needs no advice, but a wise man listens to others—*Proverbs 12:15, TLB.*

Listen to advice and accept instruction, and in the end you will be wise—*Proverbs 19:20, NIV.*

Perfume and incense bring joy to the heart, and the pleasantness of one's friend springs from his earnest counsel—*Proverbs 27:9, NIV.*

25. Don't hoard food.

People curse the man who hoards grain, but blessing crowns him who is willing to sell—*Proverbs 11:26, NIV.*

I have been young and now I am old. And in all my years I have never seen the Lord forsake a man who loves him; nor have I seen the children of the godly go hungry. Instead, the godly are able to be generous with their gifts and loans to others, and their children are a blessing—*Psalm 37:25-26, TLB.*

Look at the birds! They don't worry about what to eat—they don't need to sow or reap or store up food—for your heavenly Father feeds them. And you are far more valuable to him than they are. Will all your worries add a single moment to your life?—*Matthew 6:26-27, TLB.*

But you shouldn't be so concerned about perishable things like food. No, spend your energy seeking the eternal life that I, the Messiah, can give you. For God the Father has sent me for this very purpose—*John 6:27, TLB.*

26. Encourage people who are hurting and depressed—but do it intelligently!

Being happy-go-lucky around a person whose heart is heavy is as bad as stealing his jacket in cold weather, or rubbing salt in his wounds—*Proverbs 25:20, TLB.*

If you shout a pleasant greeting to a friend too early in the morning, he will count it as a curse!—*Proverbs 27:14, TLB.*

The mouth of the righteous man utters wisdom, and his tongue speaks what is just. The law of his God is in his heart; his feet do not slip—*Psalm 37:30-31, NIV.*

The wise man's words are like goads that spur to action. They nail down important truths. Students are wise who master what their teachers tell them—*Ecclesiastes 12:11, TLB.*

When others are happy, be happy with them. If they are sad, share their sorrow—*Romans 12:15, TLB.*

An anxious heart weighs a man down, but a kind word cheers him up—*Proverbs 12:25, NIV.*

27. Don't believe everything you hear.

A simple man believes anything, but a prudent man gives thought to his steps—*Proverbs 14:15, NIV.*

Any story sounds true until someone tells the other side and sets the record straight—*Proverbs 18:17, TLB.*

Do not entertain an accusation against an elder unless it is brought by two or three witnesses—*1 Timothy 5:19, NIV.*

Don't eavesdrop! You may hear your servant cursing you! For you know how often you yourself curse others!—*Ecclesiastes 7:21-22, TLB.*

28. Bring your temper under control before you destroy everything in your life!

A short-tempered man is a fool. He hates the man who is patient—*Proverbs 14:17, TLB.*

A wise man controls his temper. He knows that anger causes mistakes—*Proverbs 14:29, TLB.*

A hot-tempered man stirs up dissension, but a patient man calms a quarrel—*Proverbs 15:18, NIV.*

Better a patient man than a warrior, a man who controls his temper than one who takes a city—*Proverbs 16:32, NIV.*

A short-tempered man must bear his own penalty; you can't do much to help him. If you try once you must try a dozen times!—*Proverbs 19:19, TLB.*

Do not make friends with a hot-tempered man, do not associate with one easily angered, or you may learn his ways and get yourself ensnared—*Proverbs 22:24-25, NIV.*

A rebel shouts in anger; a wise man holds his temper in and cools it—*Proverbs 29:11, TLB.*

There is more hope for a fool than for a man of quick temper—*Proverbs 29:20, TLB.*

A hot-tempered man starts fights and gets into all kinds of trouble—*Proverbs 29:22, TLB.*

29. Reverence God as the one true source of character growth.

He who fears the Lord has a secure fortress, and for his children it will be a refuge. The fear of the Lord is a fountain of life, turning a man from the snares of death—*Proverbs 14:26-27, NIV.*

Humility and reverence for the Lord will make you both wise and honored—*Proverbs 15:33, TLB.*

Iniquity is atoned for by mercy and truth; evil is avoided by reverence for God—*Proverbs 16:6, TLB.*

Reverence for God gives life, happiness, and protection from harm—*Proverbs 19:23, TLB.*

Charm is deceptive, and beauty is fleeting; but a woman who fears the Lord is to be praised—*Proverbs 31:30, NIV.*

The Lord confides in those who fear him; he makes his covenant known to them—*Psalm 25:14, NIV.*

The fear of the Lord is the beginning of knowledge, but fools despise wisdom and discipline—*Proverbs 1:7, NIV.*

True humility and respect for the Lord lead a man to riches, honor and long life—*Proverbs 22:4, TLB.*

30. Develop a relaxed, joyful attitude toward life.

A relaxed attitude lengthens a man's life; jealousy rots it away—*Proverbs 14:30, TLB.*

All the days of the oppressed are wretched, but the cheerful heart has a continual feast—*Proverbs 15:15, NIV.*

A cheerful heart does good like medicine, but a broken spirit makes one sick—*Proverbs 17:22, TLB.*

May the righteous be glad and rejoice before God; may they be happy and joyful—*Psalm 68:3, NIV.*

The poor will see and be glad—you who seek God, may your hearts live!—*Psalm 69:32, NIV.*

Light is sweet, and it pleases the eyes to see the sun. However many years a man may live, let him enjoy them all. But let him remember the days of darkness, for they will be many. Everything to come is meaningless—*Ecclesiastes 11:7-8, NIV.*

O my soul, don't be discouraged. Don't be upset. Expect God to act! For I know that I shall again have plenty of reason to praise him for all that he will do. He is my help! He is my God!—*Psalm 42:11, TLB.*

31. Stay hungry for truth.

A wise man is hungry for truth, while the mocker feeds on trash—*Proverbs 15:14, TLB.*

The laborer's appetite works for him; his hunger drives him on—*Proverbs 16:26, NIV.*

Happy are those who long to be just and good, for they shall be completely satisfied—*Matthew 5:6, TLB.*

Yes, he humbled you by letting you go hungry and then feeding you with manna, a food previously unknown to both you and your ancestors. He did it to help you realize that food isn't everything, and that real life comes by obeying every command of God—*Deuteronomy 8:3, TLB.*

For he satisfies the thirsty soul and fills the hungry soul with good—*Psalm 107:9, TLB.*

If you call out for insight and cry aloud for understanding, and if you look for it as for silver and search for it as for hidden treasure, then you will understand the fear of the Lord and find the knowledge of God—*Proverbs 2:3-5, NIV.*

32. Don't try to prove you are right.

We can always "prove" that we are right, but is the Lord convinced?—*Proverbs 16:2, TLB.*

All a man's ways seem right to him, but the Lord weighs the heart—*Proverbs 21:2, NIV.*

A man who refuses to admit his mistakes can never be successful. But if he confesses and forsakes them, he gets another chance—*Proverbs 28:13, TLB.*

Like clouds and wind without rain is a man who boasts of gifts he does not give . . . . It is not good to eat too much honey, nor is it honorable to seek one's own honor—*Proverbs 25:14,27, NIV.*

Let another praise you, and not your own mouth; someone else, and not your own lips—*Proverbs 27:2, NIV.*

There is one thing worse than a fool, and that is a man who is conceited—*Proverbs 26:12, TLB.*

33. Commit everything in your life to God's care.

Commit your work to the Lord, then it will succeed—*Proverbs 16:3, TLB.*

What a God he is! How perfect in every way! All his promises prove true. He is a shield for everyone who hides behind him—*Psalm 18:30, TLB.*

Trust in the Lord and do good; dwell in the land and enjoy safe pasture. Delight yourself in the Lord and he will give you the desires of your heart—*Psalm 37:3-4, NIV.*

For the Lord God is a sun and shield; the Lord bestows favor and honor; no good thing does he withhold from those whose walk is blameless—*Psalm 84:11, NIV.*

Send me a sign of your favor. When those who hate me see it they will lose face because you help and comfort me—*Psalm 86:17, TLB.*

The lions may grow weak and hungry, but those who seek the Lord lack no good thing—*Psalm 34:10, NIV.*

34. Never gloat when your enemies suffer. Never seek revenge.

Mocking the poor is mocking the God who made them. He will punish those who rejoice at others' misfortunes—*Proverbs 17:5, TLB.*

If a man pays back evil for good, evil will never leave his house—*Proverbs 17:13, NIV.*

Do not say, "I'll pay you back for this wrong!" Wait for the Lord, and he will deliver you—*Proverbs 20:22, NIV*.

Do not gloat when your enemy falls; when he stumbles, do not let your heart rejoice—*Proverbs 24:17, NIV*.

Never pay back evil for evil. Do things in such a way that everyone can see you are honest clear through—*Romans 12:17, TLB*.

Do not say, "I'll do to him as he has done to me; I'll pay that man back for what he did"—*Proverbs 24:29, NIV*.

A quick-tempered man does foolish things, and a crafty man is hated . . . . A patient man has great understanding, but a quick-tempered man displays folly—*Proverbs 14:17,29, NIV*.

35. Look past mistakes in others.

Love forgets mistakes; nagging about them parts the best of friends—*Proverbs 17:9, TLB*.

A wise man restrains his anger and overlooks insults. This is to his credit—*Proverbs 19:11, TLB*.

Do not judge, or you too will be judged. For in the same way you judge others, you will be judged, and with the measure you use, it will be measured to you. Why do you look at the speck of sawdust in your brother's eye and pay no attention to the plank in your own eye? How can you say to your brother, "Let me take the speck out of your eye," when all the time there is a plank in your own eye? You hypocrite, first take the plank out of your own eye, and then you will see clearly to remove the speck from your brother's eye—*Matthew 7:1-5, NIV.*

Be kind and compassionate to one another, forgiving each other, just as in Christ God forgave you—*Ephesians 4:32, NIV.*

36. Always be loyal to your friends. Enjoy them.

A true friend is always loyal, and a brother is born to help in time of need—*Proverbs 17:17, TLB.*

It is harder to win back the friendship of an offended brother than to capture a fortified city. His anger shuts you out like iron bars—*Proverbs 18:19, TLB.*

A man of many companions may come to ruin, but there is a friend who sticks closer than a brother—*Proverbs 18:24, NIV.*

Most people will tell you what loyal friends they are, but are they telling the truth?—*Proverbs 20:6, TLB.*

Never abandon a friend—either yours or your father's. Then you won't need to go to a distant relative for help in your time of need—*Proverbs 27:10, TLB.*

37. Stubbornness is a satanic trait—learn to submit.

The selfish man quarrels against every sound principle of conduct by demanding his own way—*Proverbs 18:1, TLB.*

An evil man is stubborn, but a godly man will reconsider—*Proverbs 21:29, TLB.*

A man who remains stiff-necked after many rebukes will suddenly be destroyed—without remedy—*Proverbs 29:1, NIV.*

The Lord hates the stubborn but delights in those who are good—*Proverbs 11:20, TLB.*

Submit to one another out of reverence for Christ—*Ephesians 5:21, NIV.*

Rebellion is as bad as the sin of witchcraft, and stubbornness is as bad as worshiping idols—*1 Samuel 15:23, TLB.*

The mind of sinful man is death, but the mind controlled by the Spirit is life and peace; the sinful mind is hostile to God. It does not submit to God's law, nor can it do so. Those controlled by the sinful nature cannot please God—*Romans 8:6-8, NIV.*

38. Always keep an open mind.

The intelligent man is always open to new ideas. In fact, he looks for them—*Proverbs 18:15, TLB.*

A wicked man puts up a bold front, but an upright man gives thought to his ways—*Proverbs 21:29, NIV.*

The wise man is glad to be instructed, but a self-sufficient fool falls flat on his face—*Proverbs 10:8, TLB.*

The Lord hates the stubborn but delights in those who are good—*Proverbs 11:20, TLB.*

Get to know the God of your fathers. Worship and serve him with a clean heart and a willing mind, for the Lord sees every heart and understands and knows every thought. If you seek him, you will find him; but if you forsake him, he will permanently throw you aside. So be very careful, for the Lord has chosen you to build his holy temple. Be strong and do as he commands—*1 Chronicles 28:9-10, TLB.*

[The] people's minds and understanding were veiled and blinded too . . . . For this veil of misunderstanding can be removed only by believing in Christ—*2 Corinthians 3:14, TLB.*

39. Don't rush into things—go slow and be sure.

It is dangerous and sinful to rush into the unknown. A man may ruin his chances by his own foolishness and then blame it on the Lord!—*Proverbs 19:2-3, TLB.*

Get the facts at any price, and hold on tightly to all the good sense you can get—*Proverbs 23:23, TLB.*

Any enterprise is built by wise planning, becomes strong through common sense, and profits wonderfully by keeping abreast of the facts—*Proverbs 24:3-4, TLB.*

Do not boast about tomorrow, for you do not know what a day may bring forth—*Proverbs 27:1, NIV.*

What you have seen with your eyes do not bring hastily to court, for what will you do in the end if your neighbor puts you to shame?—*Proverbs 25:8, NIV.*

See the way God does things and fall into line. Don't fight the facts of nature—*Ecclesiastes 7:13, TLB.*

40. Develop a spirit of kindness.

Kindness makes a man attractive. And it is better to be poor than dishonest—*Proverbs 19:22, TLB.*

The man who tries to be good, loving and kind finds life, righteousness and honor—*Proverbs 21:21, TLB.*

A kind man benefits himself, but a cruel man brings himself harm—*Proverbs 11:17, NIV.*

Kind words are like honey—enjoyable and healthful—*Proverbs 16:24, TLB.*

When she speaks, her words are wise, and kindness is the rule for everything she says—*Proverbs 31:26, TLB.*

The fruit of the Spirit is love, joy, peace, patience, kindness, goodness, faithfulness, gentleness and self-control. Against such things there is no law—*Galatians 5:22-23, NIV.*

Since you have been chosen by God who has given you this new kind of life, and because of his deep love and concern for you, you should practice tenderhearted mercy and kindness to others—*Colossians 3:12, TLB.*

41. Never, never get involved in other people's quarrels.

It is an honor for a man to stay out of a fight. Only fools insist on quarreling—*Proverbs 20:3, TLB.*

Yanking a dog's ears is no more foolish than interfering in an argument that isn't any of your business—*Proverbs 26:17, TLB.*

To quarrel with a neighbor is foolish; a man with good sense holds his tongue—*Proverbs 11:12, TLB.*

A short-tempered man must bear his own penalty; you can't do much to help him. If you try once you must try a dozen times!—*Proverbs 19:19, TLB.*

Don't get involved in foolish arguments which only upset people and make them angry—*2 Timothy 2:23, TLB.*

Avoid foolish controversies and genealogies and arguments and quarrels about the law, because these are unprofitable and useless—*Titus 3:9, NIV.*

42. Learn to shut up and listen.

The wise man learns by listening; the simpleton can learn only by seeing scorners punished—*Proverbs 21:11, TLB.*

Keep your mouth closed and you'll stay out of trouble—*Proverbs 21:23, TLB.*

Listen, my sons, to a father's instruction; pay attention and gain understanding—*Proverbs 4:1, NIV.*

He who guards his lips guards his soul, but he who speaks rashly will come to ruin—*Proverbs 13:3, NIV.*

Let the wise listen and add to their learning, and let the discerning get guidance—*Proverbs 1:5, NIV.*

I said to myself, I'm going to quit complaining! I'll keep quiet, especially when the ungodly are around me—*Psalm 39:1, TLB.*

Lord, I am speechless before you. I will not open my mouth to speak one word of complaint—*Psalm 39:9, TLB.*

Guard your steps when you go to the house of God. Go near to listen rather than to offer the sacrifice of fools, who do not know that they do wrong. Do not be quick with your mouth, do not be hasty in your heart to utter anything before God. God is in heaven and you are on earth, so let your words be few—*Ecclesiastes 5:1-2, NIV.*

43. Learn to save.

The wise man saves for the future, but the foolish man spends whatever he gets—*Proverbs 21:20, TLB.*

A prudent man foresees the difficulties ahead and prepares for them; the simpleton goes blindly on and suffers the consequences—*Proverbs 22:3, TLB.*

The wise man looks ahead. The fool attempts to fool himself and won't face facts—*Proverbs 14:8, TLB.*

There is another serious problem I have seen everywhere—savings are put into risky investments that turn sour, and soon there is nothing left to pass on to one's son. The man who speculates is soon back to where he began—with nothing. This, as I said, is a very serious problem, for all his hard work has been for nothing; he has been working for the wind. It is all swept away. All the rest of his life he is under a cloud—gloomy, discouraged, frustrated, and angry—*Ecclesiastes 5:13-17, TLB.*

44. Avoid ungodly friends.

Don't envy godless men; don't even enjoy their company—*Proverbs 24:1, TLB.*

Fear the Lord and the king, my son, and do not join with the rebellious, for those two will send sudden destruction upon them, and who knows what calamities they can bring?—*Proverbs 24:21-22, NIV.*

Do not make friends with a hot-tempered man, do not associate with one easily angered, or you may learn his ways and get yourself ensnared—*Proverbs 22:24-25, NIV.*

Blessed is the man who does not walk in the counsel of the wicked or stand in the way of sinners or sit in the seat of mockers—*Psalm 1:1, NIV.*

I want the company of the godly men and women in the land; they are the true nobility—*Psalm 16:3, TLB.*

Let a righteous man strike me—it is a kindness; let him rebuke me—it is oil on my head. My head will not refuse it. Yet my prayer is every against the deeds of evildoers—*Psalm 141:5, NIV.*

45. Don't be envious of the prosperity of others.

Don't envy the wicked. Don't covet his riches. For the evil man has no future; his light will be snuffed out—*Proverbs 24:19-20, TLB.*

Do not let your heart envy sinners, but always be zealous for the fear of the Lord—*Proverbs 23:17, NIV.*

Do not envy wicked men, do not desire their company—*Proverbs 24:1, NIV.*

Do not fret because of evil men or be envious of those who do wrong; for like the grass they will soon wither, like green plants they will soon die away. Trust in the Lord and do good; dwell in the land and enjoy safe pasture—*Psalm 37:1-3, NIV.*

Do not be dismayed when evil men grow rich and build their lovely homes. For when they die they carry nothing with them! Their honors will not follow them. Though a man calls himself happy all through his life—and the world loudly applauds success—yet in the end he dies like everyone else, and enters eternal darkness—*Psalm 49:16-19, TLB.*

Rest in the Lord; wait patiently for him to act. Don't be envious of evil men who prosper—*Psalm 37:7, TLB.*

46. Put God's work first—above all personal needs.

Honor the Lord by giving him the first part of all your income, and he will fill your barns with wheat and barley and overflow your wine vats with the finest wines—*Proverbs 3:9-10, TLB.*

I love those who love me, and those who seek me find me . . . . Blessed is the man who listens to me, watching daily at my doors, waiting at my doorway—*Proverbs 8:17,34, NIV.*

Because the Lord is my Shepherd, I have everything I need!—*Psalm 23:1, TLB.*

Don't worry at all about having enough food and clothing. Why be like the heathen? For they take pride in all these things and are deeply concerned about them. But your heavenly Father already knows perfectly well that you need them, and he will give them to you if you give him first place in your life—*Matthew 6:31-33, TLB.*

47. Bless your enemies and harbor no ill will.

If your enemy is hungry, give him food to eat; if he is thirsty, give him water to drink—*Proverbs 25:21, NIV.*

If someone mistreats you because you are a Christian, don't curse him; pray that God will bless him—*Romans 12:14, TLB.*

I tell you: Love your enemies and pray for those who persecute you—*Matthew 5:44, NIV.*

We have worked wearily with our hands to earn our living. We have blessed those who cursed us . . . . Yet right up to the present moment we are like dirt under foot, like garbage. I am not writing about these things to make you ashamed, but to warn and counsel you as beloved children . . . . So I beg you to follow my example, and do as I do—*1 Corinthians 4:12-14,16, TLB.*

Listen, all of you. Love your enemies. Do good to those who hate you. Pray for the happiness of those who curse you; implore God's blessing on those who hurt you— *Luke 6:27-28, TLB.*

Love your enemies, do good to them, and lend to them without expecting to get anything back. Then your reward will be great, and you will be sons of the Most High, because he is kind to the ungrateful and wicked. Be merciful, just as your Father is merciful— *Luke 6:35-36, NIV.*

Love does no harm to its neighbor. Therefore love is the fulfillment of the law— *Romans 13:10, NIV.*

Bless those who persecute you; bless and do not curse.— *Romans 12:14, NIV.*

48. Control your appetites before they control you.

Like a city whose walls are broken down is a man who lacks self-control— *Proverbs 25:28, NIV.*

Death and Destruction are never satisfied, and neither are the eyes of man— *Proverbs 27:20, NIV.*

When dining with a rich man, be on your guard and don't stuff yourself, though it all tastes so good; for he is trying to bribe you, and no good is going to come of his invitation—*Proverbs 23:1-3, TLB.*

Do you like honey? Don't eat too much of it, or it will make you sick!—*Proverbs 25:16, TLB.*

Do not join those who drink too much wine or gorge themselves on meat, for drunkards and gluttons become poor, and drowsiness clothes them in rags—*Proverbs 23:20-21, NIV.*

49. Don't be fooled by flattery.

Flattery is a form of hatred and wounds cruelly.—*Proverbs 26:28, TLB.*

The purity of silver and gold can be tested in a crucible, but a man is tested by his reaction to men's praise—*Proverbs 27:21, TLB.*

In the end, people appreciate frankness more than flattery—*Proverbs 28:23, TLB.*

Flattery is a trap; evil men are caught in it, but good men stay away and sing for joy—*Proverbs 29:5-6, TLB.*

It was only with their words they followed [God], not with their hearts—*Psalm 78:36, TLB.*

50. Jealousy is cancerous; destroy it entirely.

Jealousy is more dangerous and cruel than anger—*Proverbs 27:4, TLB.*

A heart at peace gives life to the body, but envy rots the bones—*Proverbs 14:30, NIV.*

Do not envy a violent man or choose any of his ways—*Proverbs 3:31, NIV.*

Do not let your heart envy sinners, but always be zealous for the fear of the Lord—*Proverbs 23:17, NIV.*

Don't envy godless men; don't even enjoy their company—*Proverbs 24:1, TLB.*

I observed that the basic motive for success is the driving force of envy and jealousy! But this, too, is foolishness, chasing the wind—*Ecclesiastes 4:4, TLB.*

Love is very patient and kind, never jealous or envious, never boastful or proud—*1 Corinthians 13:4, TLB.*

51. Never fear what man can do to you.

Fear of man is a dangerous trap, but to trust in God means safety—*Proverbs 29:25, TLB.*

You need not be afraid of disaster or the plots of wicked men, for the Lord is with you—*Proverbs 3:25-26, TLB.*

The Lord is my rock, my fortress and my deliverer; my God is my rock, in whom I take refuge. He is my shield and the horn of my salvation, my stronghold—*Psalm 18:2, NIV.*

In God I trust; I will not be afraid. What can man do to me?—*Psalm 56:11, NIV.*

In my distress I prayed to the Lord and he answered me and rescued me. He is for me! How can I be afraid? What can mere man do to me?—*Psalm 118:5-6, TLB.*

52. Don't lie on your bed at night fretting about problems.

Have two goals: wisdom—that is, knowing and doing right—and common sense. Don't let them slip away, for they fill you with living energy, and are a feather in your cap. They keep you safe from defeat and disaster and from stumbling off the trail. With them on guard you can sleep without fear; you need not be afraid of disaster or the plots of wicked men, for the Lord is with you; he protects you—*Proverbs 3:21-26, TLB.*

I will lie down and sleep in peace, for you alone, O Lord, make me dwell in safety—*Psalm 4:8, NIV.*

You have seen me tossing and turning through the night. You have collected all my tears and preserved them in your bottle! You have recorded every one in your book. The very day I call for help, the tide of battle turns. My enemies flee! This one thing I know: God is for me!—*Psalm 56:8-9, TLB.*

I lay down and slept in peace and woke up safely, for the Lord was watching over me—*Psalm 3:5, TLB.*

53. Learn to be content with what you have.

A little, gained honestly, is better than great wealth gotten by dishonest means—*Proverbs 16:8, TLB.*

My contentment is not in wealth but in seeing you and knowing all is well between us. And when I awake in heaven, I will be fully satisfied, for I will see you face to face—*Psalm 17:15, TLB.*

Of course, it is very good if a man has received wealth from the Lord, and the good health to enjoy it. To enjoy your work and to accept your lot in life—that is indeed a gift from God. The person who does that will not need to look back with sorrow on his past, for God gives him joy—*Ecclesiastes 5:19-20, TLB.*

Though a man lives a thousand years twice over, but doesn't find contentment—well, what's the use?—*Ecclesiastes 6:6, TLB.*

Two things I ask of you, O Lord; do not refuse me before I die: Keep falsehood and lies far from me; give me neither poverty nor riches, but give me only my daily bread. Otherwise, I may have too much and disown you and say, "Who is the Lord?" Or I may become poor and steal, and so dishonor the name of my God—*Proverbs 30:7-9, NIV.*

Not that I was ever in need, for I have learned how to get along happily whether I have much or little—*Philippians 4:11, TLB.*

54. Be patient.

A hot-tempered man stirs up dissension, but a patient man calms a quarrel—*Proverbs 15:18, NIV.*

Don't be impatient. Wait for the Lord, and he will come and save you! Be brave, stout-hearted and courageous. Yes, wait and he will help you—*Psalm 27:14, TLB.*

Be still before the Lord and wait patiently for him; do not fret when men succeed in their ways, when they carry out their wicked schemes. Refrain from anger and turn from wrath; do not fret—it leads only to evil. For evil men will be cut off, but those who hope in the Lord will inherit the land—*Psalm 37:7-9, NIV.*

The end of a matter is better than its beginning, and patience is better than pride—*Ecclesiastes 7:8, NIV.*

Be joyful in hope, patient in affliction, faithful in prayer—*Romans 12:12, NIV.*

God's people must not be quarrelsome; they must be gentle, patient teachers of those who are wrong—*2 Timothy 2:24, TLB.*

55. Allow no fear in your life.

You need not be afraid of disaster or the plots of wicked men—*Proverbs 3:25, TLB.*

Fear of man is a dangerous trap, but to trust in God means safety—*Proverbs 29:25, TLB.*

He alone is my rock and my salvation; he is my fortress, I will never be shaken—*Psalm 62:2, NIV.*

Even when walking through the dark valley of death I will not be afraid, for you are close beside me, guarding, guiding all the way—*Psalm 23:4, TLB.*

The Lord is my light and my salvation—whom shall I fear? The Lord is the stronghold of my life—of whom shall I be afraid?—*Psalm 27:1, NIV.*

God did not give us a spirit of timidity, but a spirit of power, of love and of self-discipline—*2 Timothy 1:7, NIV.*

56. Think of death without fearing it.

Yes, a wise man thinks much of death, while the fool thinks only of having a good time now—*Ecclesiastes 7:4, TLB.*

The eyes of the Lord are on those who fear him, on those whose hope is in his unfailing love, to deliver them from death and keep them alive in famine—*Psalm 33:18-19, NIV.*

The godly have a refuge when they die, but the wicked are crushed by their sins—*Proverbs 14:32, TLB.*

Even when walking through the dark valley of death I will not be afraid, for you are close beside me, guarding, guiding all the way—*Psalm 23:4, TLB.*

57. If God is prospering you—don't feel guilty.

When times are good, be happy; but when times are bad, consider: God has made the one as well as the other. Therefore, a man cannot discover anything about his future—*Ecclesiastes 7:14, NIV.*

Tackle every task that comes along, and if you fear God you can expect his blessing—*Ecclesiastes 7:18, TLB.*

I know that there is nothing better for men than to be happy and do good while they live. That every man may eat and drink, and find satisfaction in all his toil—this is the gift of God—*Ecclesiastes 3:12-13, NIV.*

When God gives any man wealth and possessions, and enables him to enjoy them, to accept his lot and be happy in his work—this is a gift of God. He seldom reflects on the days of his life, because God keeps him occupied with gladness of heart—*Ecclesiastes 5:19-20, NIV.*

58. Don't judge anyone by appearances or by what he believes.

Accept him whose faith is weak, without passing judgment on disputable matters—*Romans 14:1, NIV.*

They are God's servants, not yours. They are responsible to him, not to you. Let him tell them whether they are right or wrong. And God is able to make them do as they should—*Romans 14:4, TLB.*

You have no right to criticize your brother or look down on him. Remember, each of us will stand personally before the Judgment Seat of God—*Romans 14:10, TLB.*

For the kingdom of God is not a matter of eating and drinking, but of righteousness, peace and joy in the Holy Spirit—*Romans 14:17, NIV.*

Don't criticize and speak evil about each other, dear brothers. If you do, you will be fighting against God's law of loving one another, declaring it is wrong. But your job is not to decide whether this law is right or wrong, but to obey it. Only he who made the law can rightly judge among us. He alone decides to save us or destroy. So what right do you have to judge or criticize others?—*James 4:11-12, TLB.*

59. Never criticize—that is destructive to all growth.

As a north wind brings rain, so a sly tongue brings angry looks—*Proverbs 25:23, NIV.*

There is living truth in what a good man says, but the mouth of the evil man is filled with curses—*Proverbs 10:11, TLB.*

A soft answer turns away wrath, but harsh words cause quarrels—*Proverbs 15:1, TLB.*

Gentle words cause life and health; griping brings discouragement—*Proverbs 15:4, TLB.*

A good man thinks before he speaks; the evil man pours out his evil words without a thought—*Proverbs 15:28, TLB.*

A fool gets into constant fights. His mouth is his undoing! His words endanger him—*Proverbs 18:6-7, TLB.*

60. Try to be at peace with all men.

May the God who gives endurance and encouragement give you a spirit of unity among yourselves as you follow Christ Jesus, so that with one heart and mouth you may glorify the God and Father of our Lord Jesus Christ—*Romans 15:5-6, NIV.*

Deceit fills hearts that are plotting for evil; joy fills hearts that are planning for good!—*Proverbs 12:20, TLB.*

How wonderful it is, how pleasant, when brothers live in harmony!—*Psalm 133:1, TLB.*

Blessed are the peacemakers, for they will be called sons of God—*Matthew 5:9, NIV.*

Don't quarrel with anyone. Be at peace with everyone, just as much as possible—*Romans 12:18, TLB.*

Salt is good, but if it loses its saltiness, how can you make it salty again? Have salt in yourselves, and be at peace with each other—*Mark 9:50, NIV.*

61. Keep your thought life under control.

Above all else, guard your affections. For they influence everything else in your life— *Proverbs 4:23, TLB.*

It is the thought-life that pollutes. For from within, out of men's hearts, come evil thoughts of lust, theft, murder, adultery, wanting what belongs to others, wickedness, deceit, lewdness, envy, slander, pride, and all other folly. All these vile things come from within; they are what pollute you and make you unfit for God— *Mark 7:20-23, TLB.*

We demolish arguments and every pretension that sets itself up against the knowledge of God, and we take captive every thought to make it obedient to Christ— *2 Corinthians 10:4-5, NIV.*

I am frightened, fearing that in some way you will be led away from your pure and simple devotion to our Lord, just as Eve was deceived by Satan in the Garden of Eden— *2 Corinthians 11:3, TLB.*

Whatever God says to us is full of living power; it is sharper than the sharpest dagger, cutting swift and deep into our innermost thoughts and desires with all their parts, exposing us for what we really are—*Hebrews 4:12, TLB.*

[Hold] on to faith and a good conscience. Some have rejected these and so have shipwrecked their faith—*1 Timothy 1:19, NIV.*

62. Never let the cares of this life rob you of peace.

Take your share of suffering as a good soldier of Jesus Christ, just as I do, and as Christ's soldier do not let yourself become tied up in worldly affairs, for then you cannot satisfy the one who has enlisted you in his army—*2 Timothy 2:3-4, TLB.*

Give your burdens to the Lord. He will carry them. He will not permit the godly to slip or fall—*Psalm 55:22, TLB.*

Consider how the lilies grow. They do not labor or spin. Yet I tell you, not even Solomon in all his splendor was dressed like one of these. If that is how God clothes the grass of the field, which is here today, and tomorrow is thrown into the fire, how much more will he clothe you, O you of little faith!—*Luke 12:27-28, NIV.*

Don't worry about things—food, drink, and clothes. For you already have life and a body—and they are far more important than what to eat and wear—*Matthew 6:25, TLB.*

Do not worry about tomorrow, for tomorrow will worry about itself. Each day has enough trouble of its own—*Matthew 6:34, NIV.*

63. Allow no anger to rule your spirit.

Do not be quickly provoked in your spirit, for anger resides in the lap of fools—*Ecclesiastes 7:9, NIV.*

A wise man controls his temper. He knows that anger causes mistakes—*Proverbs 14:29, TLB.*

Dear friends, never avenge yourselves. Leave that to God, for he has said that he will repay those who deserve it. (Don't take the law into your own hands.)—*Romans 12:19, TLB.*

I . . . tell you that if you are only angry, even in your own home, you are in danger of judgment! If you call your friend an idiot,

you are in danger of being brought before
the court. And if you curse him, you are in
danger of the fires of hell—*Matthew 5:22,
TLB*.

64. Keep believing that God will give you the sanctified desires of your heart.

He is close to all who call on him sincerely. He fulfills the desires of those who
reverence and trust him; he hears their cries
for help and rescues them—*Psalm 145:18-
19, TLB*.

Even strong young lions sometimes go
hungry, but those of us who reverence the
Lord will never lack any good thing—*Psalm
34:10, TLB*.

The Lord is wonderfully good to those
who wait for him, to those who seek for him.
It is good both to hope and wait quietly for
the salvation of the Lord—*Lamentations
3:25-26, TLB*.

You can never please God without faith,
without depending on him. Anyone who
wants to come to God must believe that
there is a God and that he rewards those
who sincerely look for him—*Hebrews 11:6,
TLB*.

65. Don't be afraid of failing God—or falling.

For you have saved me from death and my feet from slipping, so that I can walk before the Lord in the land of the living—*Psalm 56:13, TLB.*

The Lord upholds all those who fall and lifts up all who are bowed down—*Psalm 145:14, NIV.*

He will not let your foot slip—he who watches over you will not slumber; indeed, he who watches over Israel will neither slumber nor sleep—*Psalm 121:3-4, NIV.*

A good man has firm footing, but a crook will slip and fall—*Proverbs 10:9, TLB.*

66. Accept the forgiveness of the Lord.

He forgives all my sins. He heals me—*Psalm 103:3, TLB.*

He does not treat us as our sins deserve or repay us according to our iniquities—*Psalm 103:10, NIV.*

He is like a father to us, tender and sympathetic to those who reverence him. For he knows we are but dust—*Psalm 103:13-14, TLB.*

If you, O Lord, kept a record of sins, O Lord, who could stand? But with you there is forgiveness; therefore you are feared—*Psalm 130:3-4, NIV.*

You forgave the iniquity of your people and covered all their sins. You set aside all your wrath and turned from your fierce anger—*Psalm 85:2-3, NIV.*

67. God heals broken hearts of those who have childlike trust in Him.

He heals the brokenhearted, binding up their wounds—*Psalm 147:3, TLB.*

Though I am surrounded by troubles, you will bring me safely through them. You will clench your fist against my angry enemies! Your power will save me—*Psalm 138:7, TLB.*

The Lord is close to those whose hearts are breaking; he rescues those who are humbly sorry for their sins—*Psalm 34:18, TLB.*

The Spirit of the Lord God is upon me, because the Lord has anointed me to bring good news to the suffering and afflicted. He has sent me to comfort the broken-hearted, to announce liberty to captives and to open the eyes of the blind—*Isaiah 61:1, TLB.*

68. Convince yourself that God is hearing your prayers.

The eyes of the Lord are on the righteous and his ears are attentive to their cry—*Psalm 34:15, NIV.*

I cried out to the Lord, and he heard me from his Temple in Jerusalem—*Psalm 3:4, TLB.*

Go, leave me now, you men of evil deeds, for the Lord has heard my weeping and my pleading. He will answer all my prayers—*Psalm 6:8-9, TLB.*

In my distress I called to the Lord; I cried to my God for help. From his temple he heard my voice; my cry came before him, into his ears—*Psalm 18:6, NIV.*

Praise be to the Lord, for he has heard my cry for mercy—*Psalm 28:6, NIV.*

I spoke too hastily when I said, "The Lord has deserted me," for you listened to my plea and answered me—*Psalm 31:22, TLB.*

I cried to him and he answered me! He freed me from all my fears. Others too were radiant at what he did for them. Theirs was no downcast look of rejection! This poor man cried to the Lord—and the Lord heard him and saved him out of his troubles. For the Angel of the Lord guards and rescues all who reverence him—*Psalm 34:4-7, TLB.*

He listened! He heard my prayer! He paid attention to it! Blessed be God who didn't turn away when I was praying, and didn't refuse me his kindness and love—*Psalm 66:19-20, TLB.*

In your distress you called and I rescued you, I answered you out of a thundercloud; I tested you at the waters of Meribah—*Psalm 81:7, NIV.*

I love the Lord because he hears my prayers and answers them. Because he bends down and listens, I will pray as long as I breathe!—*Psalm 116:1-2, TLB.*

He listened to their cries and heeded their distress—*Psalm 106:44, TLB.*

69. Keep your courage up when things get bad.

Be strong and take heart, all you who hope in the Lord—*Psalm 31:24, NIV.*

O my soul, why be so gloomy and discouraged? Trust in God! I shall again praise him for his wondrous help; he will make me smile again, for he is my God!—*Psalm 43:5, TLB.*

Happy is the man who has the God of Jacob as his helper, whose hope is in the Lord his God—*Psalm 146:5, TLB.*

There is surely a future hope for you, and your hope will not be cut off—*Proverbs 23:18, NIV.*

Subject Index

SPECIAL PRICE
ORDER FORM

As you enjoy this treasury of wisdom from God's Word, you'll probably think of others—friends and loved ones—whose lives would be blessed by God's wisdom for His children.

If so, take a moment right now to order extra copies for gifts. The regular price is $2.50 each. Your special price from GRASON is 4 copies for $7.80 ($1.95 each) plus postage and handling. Any additional copies (more than 4) will cost you only $1.75 each.

☐ YES, please send me 4 copies of POCKET PROVERBS at the special price of $7.80 plus $.70 postage and handling (regularly priced at $2.50 each).

_____ Additional copies for $1.75 each.

_____

Name

_____

Address

_____

City   State   Zip

Send this order form and your payment today to:

Grason

Box 1240
Minneapolis, MN 55440

XE

GIVE A GIFT
THAT WILL LAST . . .
and have a
lasting impression